HISTORIC

COMMUNITIES

Old-Time Toys

Bobbie Kalman & David Schimpky

 Crabtree Publishing Company

www.Crabtreebooks.com

HISTORIC COMMUNITIES

Created by Bobbie Kalman

For my mother

Editor-in-Chief
Bobbie Kalman

Writing team
Bobbie Kalman
David Schimpky

Managing editor
Lynda Hale

Editors
Tammy Everts
Petrina Gentile

Consultant
Mary Niman, director of the
Detroit Antique Toy Museum

Computer design
Lynda Hale
David Schimpky

Separations and film
Dot 'n Line Image Inc.

Printer
Worzalla Publishing Company

Special thanks to:
Mary Niman and the Detroit Antique Toy Museum,
Marg Sharp and the staff of Genesee Country Museum,
Mary Wheeler and the Toy and Miniature Museum of
Kansas City, Sheila Clark and the Museum of the City of
New York, and Black Creek Pioneer Village/TRCA.

Crabtree Publishing Company

www.crabtreebooks.com   1-800-387-7650

PMB 16A
350 Fifth Avenue,
Suite 3308
New York, NY
10118

612 Welland Avenue
St. Catharines,
Ontario
Canada
L2M 5V6

73 Lime Walk
Headington,
Oxford
OX3 7AD
United Kingdom

Cataloging in Publication Data
Kalman, Bobbie, 1947-
  Old-time toys

(Historic communities series)
Includes index.
ISBN 0-86505-481-9 (library bound) ISBN 0-86505-520-3 (pbk.)
This book examines the different toys with which children played
in the nineteenth century.

1. Toys - History - 19th century - Juvenile literature. I. Schimpky,
David, 1969-   . II. Title. III. Series: Kalman, Bobbie, 1947-   .
Historic communities.

TS2301.T7 K33 1995   j688.7/2/097309034 20   LC 95-2315
                                                            CIP

Contents

Old-time toys

What are your favorite toys? Do you spend a lot of time playing with your friends? In the 1800s, children had little time to play. Most of them spent long hours working on the family farm. Farm children played with pieces of string, bits of wood, corncobs, and old wagon wheels. A fence rail and blanket could be an imaginary horse and saddle.

The toy business grows

As more people moved into rural communities, children's lives changed. Parents started buying toys for their children. The shops in the cities and towns sold a variety of playthings. Even in small villages, people could buy toys at the general store or order them from a catalog. Parents sometimes bought expensive toys to show off how wealthy they were.

Dolls made of corn husks were as well loved as any store-bought toy.

Toys for adults

Some children from well-to-do families owned toy collections, but some toys were not meant for playing. Fancy dollhouses and dolls with china heads were often only for display. Some mechanical toys were for adults with an interest in machines, not for children. Parents often found optical toys more interesting than children did. Most children preferred to play with simple toys such as blocks or pull toys.

*(left) A **whirligig** was a toy that spun around when someone pulled its string.*

*(right) The **do-nothing** toy was a wooden block with a turning crank on the top. What did it do? Nothing at all!*

The toymakers

The early settlers made everything themselves—food, clothing, tools, and even toys! Fathers and grandfathers carved dolls, model boats, and whistles from wood. Mothers and grandmothers made dolls and dolls' clothes from rags and scraps of cloth. The local carpenter sometimes made toys and sold them in the community.

Fancy toys were brought to North America from Europe. By the 1850s, however, there were several toymakers in the United States who were also selling exciting new toys. Soon, American toys were popular around the world.

(above) Charles Crandall, a famous American toymaker, produced all sorts of wooden blocks and puzzles.

In 1903, Albert Schoenhut introduced the Humpty Dumpty Circus, which became an instant success. This American toymaker also made dolls, wooden figures, and tiny toy pianos that worked just like real pianos.

George Brown was an inventor who loved making mechanical toys. In 1856, he started the George Brown Company in Forestville, Connecticut. Brown led the way in making wind-up toys, including the first wind-up trains.

The first board game produced by Milton Bradley was called The Checkered Game of Life. To meet the demand for this popular game, Bradley and an assistant worked long hours cutting, pasting, and folding the games. Milton Bradley became a successful producer of many colorful, popular games for children.

One of the first professional dollmakers in the United States was a woman named Izannah Walker. Her "unbreakable" dolls were made of stuffed fabric. They had painted features and hair.

(above) These boxes are called **nesting** blocks *because each box fits inside another. If a child took all the boxes out, he or she could make a zoo.*

(left) *The tumbling blocks of a Jacob's Ladder toy provided hours of magical entertainment.*

(below) *Budding young architects could design towers, bridges, and other amazing structures with wooden building blocks.*

Amazing blocks

Very young children played with toys such as blocks and puzzles. Blocks were educational as well as fun. Young children practiced working with their hands when they played with blocks. The sides of some blocks were decorated with letters of the alphabet, numbers, or pictures of animals. Sometimes blocks had part of a picture on one side, forming a simple puzzle. When the blocks were arranged properly, they were transformed into a colorful picture. Using blocks and some imagination, children could also create houses, castles, and towers.

Jacob's Ladder

The Jacob's Ladder toy was very popular in the late 1800s. It was made of several flat wooden blocks that were connected with ribbons. When held correctly, it looked as if one block were tumbling down over the blocks beneath it. A child could also make a chair, table, star, animals, and other shapes by holding the end blocks and moving the Jacob's Ladder with two hands.

The name "Jacob's Ladder" comes from a story in the Bible. Jacob, whose descendants became the people of Israel, was on a journey across the desert. One night, he had a dream. He saw hundreds of angels moving up and down a ladder between heaven and earth. The Jacob's Ladder toy looks and moves like a person descending a ladder.

(right) Some blocks were decorated with pictures or letters. Lettered blocks helped children learn the alphabet.

Toy animals

Like kids today, many children in the 1800s loved animals. Some favorite toys were in the shapes of familiar barnyard animals. Other toys looked like exotic animals from faraway lands.

On a wooden rocking horse, children could gallop wherever their imagination took them.

Pull toys

Children delighted in pulling about tin figures mounted on cast-iron wheels. Although vehicle pull toys, such as firefighting wagons, were popular, animals were the favorites. Horses were the most common animal pull toy.

Noah's Ark

The Noah's Ark toy was based on a Bible story. God told Noah to build a giant boat called an **ark** because a great flood was coming. Along with his family, Noah brought two of every animal onto the ark. They all survived the flood. Since the Noah's Ark toy was based on a Bible story, it was one of the few toys with which children were allowed to play on Sundays.

The toy ark looked like a house on a raft. Its roof opened so that the brightly painted wooden figures of Noah, his family, and the animals could be stored inside.

(above) Tin pull toys in the shape of circus animals were prized playthings. Both children and adults were fascinated by unusual animals from other countries.

(below) Many Noah's Ark toys were made by toymakers in Europe, although some were carved by local carpenters.

Children had many names for different kinds of marbles. Taws, aggies, cat-eyes, swirls, and onionskins were just a few. The large glass marble in the center of this picture has a figure inside. This type of marble is called a **sulphide.**

Schoolyard toys

At school, children were allowed to play during recess and lunchtime. Many brought toys to school so they could share them with their friends. Hoops, marbles, jacks, and tops were all favorite schoolyard toys.

Marbles

Marbles were made of stone, pottery, clay, or china. Some had colorful swirls or strange designs. Children who had no marbles used musketballs, nuts, or hard berries to play instead.

Marble collections were always changing, as children won, lost, and traded their marbles. A big bag of marbles was considered a treasure. Losing at marbles was very disappointing. Perhaps the expression "lost their marbles" began as a description of an angry loser!

Jacks

The game of jacks was played with small, six-pronged objects called **jackstones**, or **jacks**. The first player started the game by throwing the jackstones on the ground. The other players then took turns tossing one jack into the air, picking up another jack from the ground, and then catching the flying jack as it came back down—all with the same hand!

In the next rounds, players tried to grab two jacks, then three, then four. If someone failed to pick up enough jacks, or allowed the flying jack to hit the ground, that person was out of the game. In the late 1800s, players bounced a rubber ball instead of throwing a jack in the air.

Jacks, played with or without a rubber ball, was a favorite schoolyard game. It required skill and good reflexes.

Tops

Tops were favorite toys with both boys and girls. They came in many different styles. Some were wound up with a string. Others had a long, round stem for spinning. **Peg tops** were the most common kind of top. They were made of a single carved piece of wood. A **humming top** was hollow and had a hole in one side. When it spun, it made a whistling or humming noise.

Conqueror was an exciting game. Two players spun their tops so that the tops bounced against each other. The top that knocked the other over, while staying upright itself, was the winner. In other games, competitors tried to spin a top onto a target or see whose top could spin the longest.

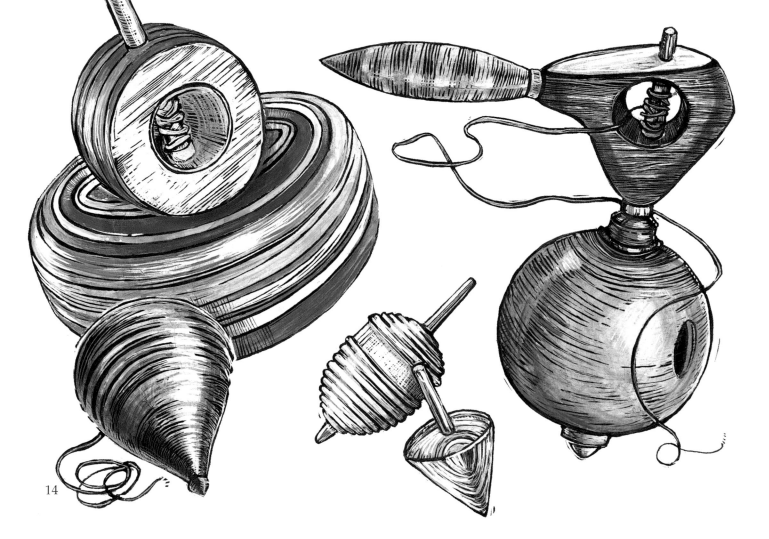

14

Hoops

A wooden or metal hoop could provide hours of fun. Boys and girls raced their hoops across the schoolyard. In order to keep the hoops upright, children guided them with a stick. Contests were held to test hoop-rolling skills. Sometimes participants had to guide their hoops through obstacle courses. In other contests, children tried to keep several hoops rolling at once.

The village cooper made hoops to hold his barrels together. When a barrel wore out, children used the hoops for their games.

(From left to right) A doll with a china head from the 1850s, a doll with a wooden head from 1825, an Izannah Walker doll made in 1873, and a wax-headed doll from the 1860s are examples of typical nineteenth century dolls. Most dolls looked like adult women. Baby dolls were less common.

Dolls

Parents encouraged their daughters to play with dolls so they could practice being good mothers. Girls also tested their sewing skill by making dolls' clothes.

Homemade dolls

In rural areas, people fashioned dolls out of the materials at hand. Some carved dolls from pieces of wood or sewed rag dolls from cloth or deerskin. Doll heads were sometimes made from dried apples. "Apple dolls" resembled very old, wrinkled people. Even cornhusks could be bent and tied to make a doll!

A variety of dolls

Toymakers created a variety of dolls in the 1800s. Most looked like adults. Dolls that resembled babies were not made until the late 1800s.

Most dolls had wooden bodies. Many had joints at the elbows, hips, and knees so that children could bend their arms and legs. Doll heads were made of wood, papier-mâché, wax, or china. Dolls with wax heads were the most costly. They had glass eyes and natural-looking hair. Some even had real human hair!

Fashionable dolls

Some doll clothes were simple, but others were quite fancy, with ribbons, ruffles, and lace. Sometimes a doll was so beautifully dressed that its owner was only allowed to play with it on Sunday—and then only with clean hands. Some dolls were not to be touched by children at all!

A favorite doll was like a member of the family. It even had a bed of its own.

Paper dolls were first made in America in 1812, but they did not become popular until the mid-1800s. Children cut out the dolls and clothes from special books.

Dollhouses had tiny dishes, vases, clocks, candlesticks, and carpets.

The grocer's shop, butcher shop, and post office were favorite rooms, but the kitchen was the most popular doll room.

Dollhouses

A girl who owned a dollhouse was fortunate indeed! Dollhouses were among the fanciest toys available in the 1800s. They were filled with miniatures that looked like the furniture found in real houses. In the late 1800s, some dollhouses had plumbing and electric lights that really worked!

Dollhouses were built in many styles—cottages, townhouses, and mansions. Some dollhouses looked just like the homes in which their young owners lived!

A room for the dolls

Instead of having a dollhouse, some children owned a single room in which their dolls could live or work. Parents hoped that playing with miniature rooms would help their children become good shopowners or housekeepers.

This fancy dollhouse was made in the 1890s. The back of the dollhouse was open so that children could play with the objects inside. The front of the house (shown in the top right photo) had doors, windows, and a fence.

Toys on the go

*(above) The first toy trains did not travel on tracks. They were called **carpet runners** because they moved on the floor.*

(below) The warship Columbia was made of paper and wood. It came in pieces, which had to be put together by parents.

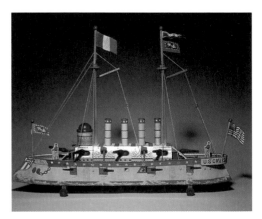

In the 1800s, there were many new and exciting ways to travel. Steamboats cruised down rivers. Trains raced across the country. Children loved to play with toys that showed both traditional and new ways of traveling.

The first toy trains were made in the 1850s. Most of them had to be pushed across the floor by hand. Some trains, however, had wind-up mechanisms or real steam engines that made them move! In the late 1800s, toy trains traveled on small tracks.

Some travel toys were life-sized! Sleds had long, curved runners and a raised board for sitting or lying. Children could zoom down snowy hills at very high speeds.

(above) The first settlers fought fires with buckets of water. By the late 1800s, fire brigades with horse-drawn wagons were used to put out fires. The brave firefighters were admired by children. Miniature fire brigades became popular toys.

(left) In the mid-1800s, skating became a popular activity. Children strapped ice skates to their boots and were ready to go!

Action books

In the early 1800s, the only books children read were their schoolbooks and the family Bible. The first fun-to-read books were created in the 1850s. They had colorful pictures and lively stories.

Action books had parts that moved! Pulling a ribbon could make a bird "fly" across the page or make a musician seem to strum a banjo. Some books came with cutout figures that fit into slots on the page. Using the figures and backgrounds, the reader could create his or her own picture and story.

A German puppeteer named Lothar Meggendorfer created some of the most famous pop-up books. His book Internationaler Circus *has six very detailed scenes in it. This scene contains an audience of 450 separate pop-up figures! Many of Meggendorfer's books were sold in North America.*

Transformation books

One of the first action books was
the **transformation book**, which was also called
an **overlay book**. A head on the last page of the
book popped through the hole that was cut out
on each page that came before. When the page
turned, the head appeared on a different body
and in a new scene.

Pop-up books

Pop-up books were first made to be enjoyed
by adults, but they soon became very popular
with children. As the reader turned a page,
a three-dimensional scene "popped up" right
before his or her eyes.

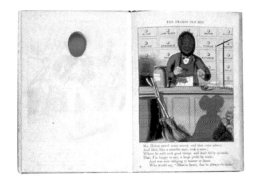

*The most popular transformation
books were made by a company
called Dean & Son. This company
was one of the first publishers of
children's action books.*

*The first **sand toys** were made in France and Germany. This toy was manufactured in the United States in the 1870s. A hidden mechanism moves the dancer's arms and legs.*

*The **jack-in-the-box** was designed to surprise children. As they turned a crank on the side of a colorfully decorated box, they could never be sure when a scary or funny-looking head would pop out!*

Automata

Toys with parts that moved on their own were called **automata**. Automata were very popular in the late 1800s. Their mechanisms were complicated and required a great deal of skill to design. Toymakers created many different kinds of automata.

Sand toys

The **sand toy** was one of the first automata. It consisted of a flat wooden box with a piece of glass on the front. Painted scenes and figures, such as acrobats, dancers, or windmills, were behind the glass. Hidden inside the sand toy was a large wheel. As sand trickled onto the paddles of the wheel, the wheel turned. The turning wheel made the figures in the scene move.

Gears and springs

Automata were sometimes called **clockwork toys** because the mechanisms used were similar to wind-up clocks. Most had small gears and springs that made the toy move. When wound up with a key, a clockwork toy could move on its own for a short time. Clockwork mechanisms made a toy animal walk, a toy man row a boat, or a toy acrobat spin on a bar!

Children's banks

Mechanical banks were popular toys in the late 1800s and early 1900s. Parents liked these banks because they made saving money fun for children. Most of these banks were made of heavy cast iron.

(left) To make this Boy Scout Camp bank work, a child placed a coin in a slot in the tree, then pressed a lever located below the owl. The coin fell into the bank, causing the Boy Scout to raise the flag above his head.

Put a penny on the clown's head, flip a switch, and—whoopee—he does a handstand that deposits the coin inside the bank. He stays upside down until he is pushed down into his original position.

Optical toys

The word "optical" means "having to do with seeing." Optical toys use light, mirrors, and movement to play tricks on the eyes. They were originally created for adults but soon became popular with children as well.

Kaleidoscope

The **kaleidoscope** was invented in 1818. It looks like a telescope, but you can see a wonderful design inside the tube. This effect is created by several mirrors at the end of the tube. The mirrors reflect the pattern made by many chips of colored glass. The design can be changed by turning the section containing the bits of glass.

Magic lantern

The **magic lantern** was similar to a modern slide projector. Instead of using an electric bulb for illumination, it used a candle or oil lamp. Slides made of glass were placed in front of the light. Each slide had a different picture painted on it. When light shone through the slide, the picture was magnified onto a screen or wall.

*Peering through a **kaleidoscope**, a child could see wonderful patterns, such as the one at the top of the page.*

Zoetrope

The **zoetrope** made pictures seem as if they were moving! This toy was a drumlike cylinder lined with a series of pictures. Between each picture was a small slot. To use the zoetrope, a child spun the cylinder and peered through a slot. The pictures inside appeared to move, creating a short cartoon. Zoetropes showed acrobats tumbling, couples dancing, and boxers fighting.

Thaumatrope

The **thaumatrope** was a stiff, round paper disk with a string on two ends. A different picture was drawn on each side of the disk. When it was spun quickly, the pictures seemed to come together. If a picture of a bird were painted on one side and a cage on the other, the spinning thaumatrope would make the bird appear to be inside the cage. Follow the instructions on page 30 and make your own thaumatrope.

(above) The **stereoscope** *was a popular optical toy. When viewed through a special eyepiece, the pair of photographs on the special cards formed one three-dimensional image.*

(below) The amazing **zoetrope** *kept children entertained for hours. If a child got bored, the picture strip inside the zoetrope could be replaced with a new set of "moving pictures."*

Board games

Chess, checkers, and backgammon have been pastimes for older children and adults for hundreds of years. In the 1800s, new board games became popular. They were designed to be played by the entire family.

Teetotum

When people played board games in settler times, they did not use dice because dice were associated with gambling. Instead, they used a **teetotum**—a top with numbers along the side. When the teetotum stopped spinning and fell on its side, the number facing up was the number of moves the player was allowed to make.

*The six-sided **teetotum** has been used instead of a die for hundreds of years. Teetotums were made of many materials, such as ivory, bone, or wood.*

Morality games

Board games had themes that were supposed to improve children's minds. For example, in Snakes and Ladders, the ladder squares had pictures of children doing good deeds. When a player landed on one of these squares, he or she moved several spaces ahead. The snake squares had pictures of children being disobedient. The player who landed on one of these was sent back several squares.

Educational games

Some board games were educational. They drilled players on subjects like science, literature, and history. Some of the most popular games, such as Round the World and Geographical Lotto, taught geography skills. Games such as Picture Lotto and Familiar Objects were designed to teach younger children words and objects. The World's Educator was a challenging game for older players.

(above) Some games were played just for fun. This board game has an upright board and uses marbles. It is similar to a modern pinball game.

(left) Some board games had religious themes. The Mansion of Happiness taught that good behavior would lead to a place in heaven.

Make a thaumatrope

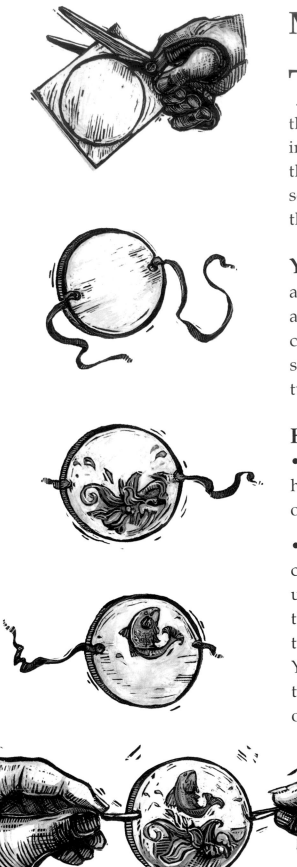

The thaumatrope works because of a principle called "persistence of vision." According to this principle, your eye continues to "see" an image for a moment after it has disappeared. The thaumatrope spins faster than your eye works, so you can "see" the pictures on both sides at the same time.

You will need:

a square piece of cardboard
a pencil
colored pencils or markers
scissors
two pieces of string

How to make it:

• Cut a circle out of the cardboard. Punch two holes on opposite edges of the circle. Tie a piece of string through each hole.

• Draw and color a picture on each side of the circle. To make sure that the pictures will match up, flip the circle bottom-side up. The picture on the second side should appear right-side up. The two pictures should create one whole picture. You can draw a bride on one side and a groom on the other or a flower on one side and a pot on the other. Use your imagination!

• When the thaumatrope is finished, hold the strings in your hands and wind up the circle tightly. Then release the circle and watch it spin and form one picture, such as the one shown here.

Glossary

architect A person who designs and supervises the construction of houses and other buildings

ark A large, flat-bottomed boat

backgammon A board game in which the moves are determined by rolling dice

carpenter An artisan who makes or builds things from wood

cast iron A hard, heavy iron mix that has been shaped in a mold

chess A board game in which two players use strategy to win each other's playing pieces

china Fine, easily breakable pottery that has been baked at a high temperature

cooper A person who makes barrels

descendant Someone who is related to a person who lived before

fire brigade A group that fights fires

gears A thin wheel with pointed teeth around it. As a gear turns, its teeth catch teeth on other gears and turn them.

Israel A country in the Middle East

mechanism The working parts of a machine

musketball A lead ball used as a bullet in an old-fashioned gun called a musket

papier-mâché A substance made of paper pulp and shreds of paper mixed with glue

pottery Items made of dried clay, usually baked in an oven called a kiln

rural Of or relating to the countryside

steamboat A kind of boat that is powered by a steam engine

three-dimensional Having height, width, and depth

warship A ship built for use in war

Index

Acknowledgments

Photographs
Marc Crabtree: pages 6 (both), 7 (all),
   8 (top, bottom right), 9, 11 (top), 15, 16,
   20-21 (all), 24 (bottom), 25 (all),
   27, 29 (both)
Bobbie Kalman: page 8 (bottom left)
Chuck Kidd/Old Sturbridge Village: page 28
Steven Mays/Rebus (Collection of
   Margaret and Blair Whitton):
   pages 17 (bottom), 22-23 (all)
Black Creek Pioneer Village/TRCA: page 31
Thomas Neill/Old Sturbridge Village:

title page, page 17 (top)
George Ross: pages 3, 12, 18 (top), 24 (top)
David Schimpky: pages 4, 5 (both), 14
Toy and Miniature Museum of Kansas City:
   pages 11 (bottom), 18 (bottom), 19 (both)

Illustrations and colorizations
Barb Bedell: cover
Tammy Everts: page 27
Sarah Pallek: title page, pages 13, 14, 26,
28, 30
David Schimpky: page 10

8 9 0   Printed in the U.S.A.   4 3 2 1